vigils for dead

Deborah

Published by Nine Pens Press
2023
www.ninepens.co.uk

ISBN: 978-1-7391517-7-5
021

for the girls who didn't make it,
and the rest of us still here and hoping

for the girls who

turned up an hour early or a day late
wore a sparkly dress to casual pub drinks
kissed the wrong person then kissed them again

gave a three-paragraph answer to *how are you?*
carried five red lipsticks but no tampons
cried at the office Christmas party

asked for triple vodka at a wine reception
sang out-of-tune power ballads at karaoke
started a fight and stormed out of the room

forgot to do laundry and went commando
answered 'both' to *cream or ice-cream?*
went all the way in the park after closing time

ate everything or nothing all night long
got no answer fifty times and kept dialling
sat down in the road and refused to get up

I see you
I've got you
We're going to be ok

when you call that girl a hot mess

know / that beneath her red lip / laddered tights / cocked hip /
drunken nights / she lives with things you do not understand /
her head a cupboard of snakes / in her bed / serpents' mistakes
/ a waste bin / it's so bad / blame / sin / it's so sad / shame /
spiral / out of control / pull the coiled rope / of this tangled web
/ woven by the reptile inside / keep pulling that thread / viper
venom keeps coming / coming / in an infinite loop / it's a sick
joke / looking for the end / looking for neat / and tidy / is only a
masquerade / the room seems clean / but the doors do not close
/ on this closet / rammed with too much / stuff / that should
have been cleared out / years ago / but has been shoved back
in / again and again / until simply bursting / with the opposite
of pride / uncontainable / - / excess / - / excess mess / the
antidote to poison / a different toxin / freshly painted is
simply a cover up / the marks cannot be removed / they can
only be coloured over / the handprints remain / underneath /
always / *will these hands ne'er be clean?* / no scrubbing / scouring
/ sage / will cleanse / is to clean / is next to godliness / may god
forgive what is spilled / and who is spoiled / stained / sullied /
shamed / mess is shame / shame / shame the devil / tell the
truth / expose to the light / but this is no vampire to be defeated
with sunshine / garlic / sign of the cross / your heart / breaks to
see / broken pieces / in every cell crevice / can you see now? /
her space was too small / to hold these multitudes / not small
enough to disappear / the memory / entire / galaxies within / all
of them incomplete / and unknowable / and burn it down / and
start over / is a tantalising dream / so there is/ only / this / mess

at the hospital for ill fairy tales

Red won't take off her cloak
her basket is always packed
ready to run, won't be fooled again
if I close my eyes I still see his teeth
shh... it's safe, no wolves here, dear
increase to 10mg of haloperidol

Snow is desperate to get home
they can't manage without her
have to check the apples again
everything I want turns to poison
shh... it's safe, you can eat here, pet
let's try you on the risperidone

Beauty is hiding in the corner
she won't take her eyes off the door
tried so hard to be good and kind
he just gave me to that... that beast
shh... it's safe, they're gone, flower
we'll add in some amitriptyline

God is silent, verging on catatonic
incapacitated by consequences
going round the free-will loop again
I could end it all and start over
shh... learn to live with yourself, love
there's nothing else we can give you

reserves

I used to hold my rounded stomach before
going to sleep, taking comfort
in its softness, its pliability and warmth.
Once a child grew there, two in fact.
But after that, only layers of self-
soothing, good times, and an increasing
unwillingness to say no to pleasure
wherever I could find it,
within ever-limited category options.

Now as I lie on my side, my hip bone
creating an uncomfortable pressure
on the bed, newly hard, like my thighs,
spinning like the miller's daughter.
Not for straw into gold, the end product
coveted is the gap, my reward thin air.
I touch what is left but I feel what is gone
from around me, like an aura of absence
now carrying the weight of expectations.

kitsune

I see him every morning at 6am, our eyes meet.
He looks a little guilty to be caught there, still out
from the evening before, a long night of hunting,
scavenging, and of generally fucking shit up.
I always smile and say hi with no judgment
because although I'm on my way to a virtuous pursuit
it's still very early, and I simply haven't started my day
of generally fucking shit up yet. He looks at me
as if he understands this, and is briefly mollified.
We watch each other for a couple of minutes
not breaking our glances, though he is less needy than I
and always tires of our interaction first, places to be,
to sleep soundly, sated by adventure, by the carnage
he leaves behind. He makes me want to do shots
of tequila, blow off the gym, and go dancing.

high force

I bring everyone I love here to this waterfall of mine
we sit on the big flat rock, the one I always sat on to read
when I was the earlier version of the one you have here now

I tell you this, kind of
and we sit side by side watching the water

falling forcefully, over and over
the rocks and I worn
from decades of this

current plunging into gorge for thousands of years
these rocks, some say
date back over 300 million years
or maybe it just feels that way sometimes

not today, sitting here, leaning into you
the roar of the cascade surging optimistically forward
and the repetition of the flow
a magician's pocket watch
fixing me

put your arms around me

I decide not to tell you things
like about the time, years before you visited
when the Beast came, and turned this force to ice

four songs

But evil shall come upon you
Which you will not know how to charm away
Disaster shall fall upon you
For which you will not be able to atone
And ruin shall come upon you suddenly
Of which you know nothing

I'm twenty-two years old. I am a shiny treasure
and you are the jackdaw about to take me
as if I was just the foil from a kit-kat wrapper
or a little piece of broken mirror.
An entirely inconsequential theft.
A brief diversion, four songs worth.

My shift at the internet café is done.
I lock the door, shut off the coffee machine,
cash up and wipe down the tables. You're here,
waiting for me to finish so we can exchange gifts
and say goodbye for Christmas. It's December 23rd.

The music has stopped, so I put on another CD
to soundtrack my closing up.
I choose one you like, *White Ladder*,
the first notes ascending, as I'm descending
the stairs to the basement where the computers are.
You're behind me, which is fine
because this is not the music for a horror film,

it's David Gray.

The first song is five and a half minutes long
and by the time we get to the end of it I'll be gone
but now it's just the beginning and I'm singing along.

<u>track 1: please forgive me</u>

please forgive me if I act a little strange, for I know not what I do

Too soon, it hasn't happened yet and you never do say this.
You never admit or acknowledge you did this.
But nevertheless, I understand and mitigate
and if that's forgive, I do. Too soon.
But we're skipping ahead too far
and the weeping prophet is waiting for us.

Thus says the Lord
Behold, I will stir up the spirit of a destroyer against Babylon

You ask me if I want to and I don't, so I say
I'm tired from a long shift.
I have a big drive ahead.
I don't want to delay setting off.
I need to get on the road.
I want to just finish up and go.

help me out here, all my words are falling short

Nicely. No.
Nicely. I don't want to.

You do
but I don't know how much yet
and I don't know that's the only factor that matters
and I don't know because there is no warning in the air
because the music still isn't at all scary, it's David Gray
as I'm reaching across the desks to turn off the computers.

throw a stone and watch the ripples flow

And then I do know. Or rather, I begin to.

You're behind me. It's a joke. No, it's not a joke.
But seriously is it? The air turns mountain thin
and now I do know, this is actually happening

I got half a mind to scream out loud

and I can only look at the screen in front of me
shutting down.

I got half a mind to die

Freeze.
Screen. Skin. Time. Limbs. Thoughts. Screen.
Freeze.

track 2: babylon

Gate of the gods.
Access to the divine.

all the lights are changing green to red

You are my hammer and weapon of war
With you I break nations in pieces
With you I destroy kingdoms

Spinning wheel.
Blue screen.
Little light.
Off switch.
Within reach.
Out of reach.

if you want it, come and get it, for crying out loud

Set a rhythm. Take your time. Get into your stride.

The warriors of Babylon have ceased fighting
They remain in their strongholds
Their strength has failed
They have become women
Her dwellings are on fire
Her bars are broken

Relax.

The daughter of Babylon is like a threshing floor

Relax.

let go of your heart, let go of your head, feel it now

Don't feel it. Don't. Don't is such a small word:
the opposite of do, a contraction of do not.
Contraction is smaller,
and this don't is too small to be viable
in a future formality that would never happen,
but not too tiny to be heard
because you did hear it, just now and before.
You did. But you did not
(didn't) care.

track 3: my oh my

what on earth is going on in my heart as it turns as cold as stone

I think I know what this mark on the wall is.
A few days ago I had come into work to a strange sound.
I went downstairs and found a bird in the basement.
It had come in and then couldn't find its way back out.
I have no idea how long it had been trapped in this room,
trying, flying this way and that
looking for an exit, but finding none.

'cause my oh my, you know it just don't stop
it's in my mind, I want to tear it up
been trying to fight it, trying to turn it off, but it's not enough

I saved it. No.
I opened the window and helped it see how to escape.
I watched it fly away.
But no one is coming tonight. It's Christmas.
And it's too late.

The king of Babylon
Has devoured me
He has crushed me
He has made me an empty vessel
He has swallowed me like a monster
He has filled his stomach with my delicacies
He has rinsed me out

track 4: we're not right

feel the weight, I've been passing time

Counting time.
Counting songs.
Counting marks.
Counting you.
Counting faster.
And it's done.

You release me.
The new me.
Not the one who stays pinned down.
Leave her. Forget her.
Leave her, it's too late.
I turn off the rest of the computers
and I turn off the light in the basement.
Everything is shut down now.
As I go up the stairs, you're behind me.
The music is louder and the lights are brighter.

I see this world, I can't relate

I turn them off.
These last rituals. I unlock the door.
You wait, standing guard while I set the alarm.
You check the street as I lock up, just in case.
You walk me to my car to be safe, as it's dark.
It's only two days after the shortest day.
Funny how we don't call it the longest night.
Maybe we save that for nights like this
that never really end.
You give me a gift and look at me expectantly.
The person I was yesterday had wrapped a gift
for the person you were yesterday
and it's here in my bag, so what else would I do
but give it to you, so I do.

You kiss me and wish me a safe journey.

I wish you a happy Christmas. You leave.
I get in the car and watch you go out of sight
like I did with the bird, unharmed, taking flight,
a lightness in your step, as though you took all
the weight that was inside you and handed it over.

I have a long road ahead of me
and I have no idea what that really means yet.
I just know I have to drive for four hours now to get home.
Whatever that can mean again.

Babylon shall become a heap of ruins
The haunt of jackals
A horror and a hissing
Without inhabitant

I'm alone in the car.
There is no one in the car.

I drive.
I don't play music.
I always play music.
I have just four hours to be fine for Christmas.
So I choose to be fine now.

B.C. to A.D.

A new world of post-apocalyptic fiction.

Her cities have become a horror
A land of drought and a desert
A land in which no one dwells

I'm twenty-two years older now
which means I've lived with your oil spill on my feathers
for as long as I didn't, in the great before.

Before words were nothing.

For the Lord is laying Babylon waste
And stilling her mighty voice

Before I learned to always say yes.

The broad wall of Babylon
Shall be levelled to the ground
And her high gates
Shall be burned with fire

Before every intimacy became a battlefield.
Where I fight myself.
And you.
And them. And you.
And my thoughts.
And my body.
Where the victories are hard won.
If they come at all.

Before every
snapped twig
slammed door
raised voice
crossed line

became simultaneously
what I did not see coming
and yet was somehow waiting for.

I understand now that I was primed to take your weight
and wear it like a rucksack, until I would entirely forget
that it didn't belong to me.

And you will not know my name now,
for who would remember kit-kat wrapper foil
or a bit of broken mirror they picked up decades before?

It's a glittering illusion, how one thing
can mean nothing, or everything
depending on who is holding it
and how you turn it to the light.
It looks like magic, but it's science,
like force and energy and strength.
Like how much weight a person can bear.

And experimenting with the distracting things
you think might make it easier to carry, and they do
for a while, but there are no shortcuts on this journey,

and the backstory of every superhero is just
exposures to different kinds of luck.
The magic is irrelevant. There is no magic.

It was not magic.

My shine was not an enchantment.
This was not a supernatural event.
It was not predetermined by the Lord
as a punishment for anyone's apostasy.
And what felt like predestination
was just swimming around in patriarchy
for so long the water felt warm.

It is not magic.

There is no superhuman strength.
Just a person who helped the bird escape the basement
and went back later for the girl she left behind.

It is not magic.

There is no unbreakable curse.
Only the things I allowed to be imbued with too much power
for too long.

Like you
and God
and David Gray.

the morning we cast you out over brunch

It started the same as most other Sundays…
Hecate and Kali drinking coffee, black as you please,
Ishtar and Eoestre ordering eggs cooked two ways,
Artemis and I just shooting the breeze.

We were still waiting for Nemesis to appear
when your name came up, really out of the blue.
I didn't mean to get into it, but of course it was clear
there was a story. They had questions - wouldn't you?

When I finished, with a flash, the electricity blew
plunging the basement into total pitch-dark.
We already had candles, a round table for our brew,
so it seemed silly *not* to hex you, someone remarked.

Some little flames, chants, gestures, just the basic skills
needed to cast you out quickly while waiting for refills.

dear _____

My therapist told me to picture you as a scorpion
in a guided meditation, in which she had me imagine -
in a very visceral way - crushing you to death
with my foot, till you were nothing but shit and dust.
Now I know what you are thinking:
surely a real therapist would never suggest such a thing!

but to be totally honest with you
she is somewhat unconventional in her methods
and only the week before this
she had asked me to imagine finding a grave
and looking down to see your lifeless body
in the deep and open dirt -

the knowledge of your death
giving me back my own breath
which I had been holding all these months
terrified that I could see you on every corner
your dark hair swinging behind you
in front of me

a kind of ponytail PTSD.
I wish I was joking.
Anyway, back to you as a scorpion, did you know
it's said they are viciously venomous for no reason?
Have you heard that fable about the frog and the scorpion?
that ends with the scorpion saying, *it's in my nature?*

Well, I don't believe that shit.
I don't believe you were born like that
to sting for the sake of it. But it doesn't matter
because you are that now
and you should be approached with extreme caution
and protective clothing, if at all

and I learned the hard way
that anyone who would keep a scorpion for a pet
is a fool. There's an urban myth
that if you light a circle of fire around a scorpion
it will sting itself to death
horribly... for a long time

I thought about how I could set your world on fire:
trap you in a prison with only your own poison
for company, and glass walls and spotlights
for all to see who you really are.
I texted your name so often
that my phone still wants to gift it to me in autocorrect

whenever I type the first three letters
but this is progress, because for a while just the E would do it.
One day I hope I can look at your name
in black and white
or even meet someone else
with it, and not hate them on sight

and though today is not that day
I know it must be coming.
I don't think of you so much now
and I wear a scorpion earring.
Not every day
but on those mornings where I wake up shaking

or when the offence of an injustice
is simply overwhelming.
It helps remind me that it's ok
if a battle is too bloody to fight,
that self-care sometimes means you don't get to win
even when you're right

and the day I grew up
is the day I understood
that the sun shines just the same
on evil and good.
Ah, scorpion…
despite all I learned about you

it's not in my nature
to claim you have no path to salvation
but it does bring me comfort to know
that at any moment
any enemy can be crushed
if only in imagination.

pick your battle!

You are walking home from the tube. A man crosses the street to your side, comes up behind you, puts his hand between your legs, then walks away at speed in front of you. You...

1. apologise Britishly in an automatic response to being 'bumped into', before realising you were sexually assaulted. By then he's gone. You go home crying.

2. chase after him and give him a piece of your mind. He laughs, tells you to fuck off, and walks away. You go home, punch a wall, and hurt your hand.

3. go to therapy, talk about all the other times and wonder if it's something about you.

4. yell to everyone else on the street, 'Stop that man! He just assaulted me!'. Everyone ignores you. He gets away. You never tell anyone about it again.

5. shout 'who the fuck do you think you are, loser?'. He comes back, and drags you into a side street, where he rapes and beats you, leaving you for dead.

6. do nothing, but see him again that night. He apologises. Then you wake up.

7. feel scared every time you go out in case it happens again. You stop going out so much, and never alone at night. It's safer to stay at home.

8. call the police. They say they can't help, while you look at the CCTV camera overhead and they look at your skirt. They tell you to call Victim Support.

9. call the police. They take your statement. They find him and arrest him. He tells them it was consensual. They laugh, say they believe him and let him go.

10. chase after him, pulling the fountain pen from your bag as you do so. You catch up with him and plunge the pen into the side of his neck, hitting the jugular vein. Blood spurts everywhere, and he quickly loses consciousness. He dies. The police come, you get arrested, charged, tried, and go to prison.

11. call your friend, mouth off about the patriarchy, go home and go to sleep.

12. think you're fine, but then you snap at your male colleague's 'banter' the next day in the office. You get a written warning for telling him to *just fuck off.*

13. write a poem about it that ends like this.

I hope it still writes okay

dressed in pink satin black belt cinched
tightly over gently swelling body
impossibly smooth silver hardware
accenting highlights drawing attention
from nib to bottom the full package
creating compulsion to touch
commanding almost silently *asking for it*

I am not afraid
of the dark
ink flowing beneath
this shiny surface
I am not afraid
of making a mark
or making a mess
on any clean surface
I am not afraid
to get the job done
force the point home
through a soft surface

if not mightier than more handbag-friendly
appropriate defence defensible legally
blonde hair framing wide eyes *oh, officer!*
I panicked and grabbed the first thing to hand!
as we both look blush pink
length still protruding obscenely
proud words remaining unspoken

to the Met officer on duty tonight

If you must find my corpse in the road, or the ditch,
please let my outstretched hand still be clutching
my keys for dear life, splayed through my fingers,
so you can nod in respect, *at least she was trying.*

Don't forget to note my boyfriend jeans, my trainers:
flat and able to run; the high visibility of my jacket -
the reflective strips which made me easier to spot.
For him. But now for you too! I'm so glad I could help.

Oh, I think you'll be switchtracked for a while
by all the scratches on my hands and arms,
until you hear I was making a Christmas wreath
with berries and foliage from my own garden!
I laughed then that 'it's not messy, it's *artisanal*'
but the one I get next will be made by an expert.

You won't be able to help puffing yourself up,
on the TV interview at first, and at parties for ever.
Do you remember this case? The hushed awe as you tell…
And with your colleagues, apart from that one text
where you made fun of my underwear (and by the way
hey! mean! I didn't know anyone would be seeing it!)
you mainly afford me some honour with your pity:
Poor bitch. Mum. Nice family. Didn't deserve that.

wear black, bring flowers

We have so many vigils now
we're introducing dress codes just to mix it up.
Sarah. Sabina. Ashling.
Don't worry if you forget these names.
Dead women are like buses,
except you don't wait for ages
and then three come along at once.
Bibaa. Nicole. Zara.
All these buses and never one to wave down.

What are you expecting this will achieve?
he asks, as he watches me carefully
cutting out my circle of cardboard
from the most recent Amazon box
expertly piercing a star in the centre
to hold my candle, already half-burned
from the one before.

Nothing, I reply, as I check my look in the mirror
funeral-casual: black jeans and jumper
hand holding my red supermarket carnations
in anticipation of laying them down
when I'm there, alongside the other useless tributes
on the ground, covered in plastic
waiting to rot in the rain.

Nothing. Obviously. Absolutely nothing.

But what are you hoping for?
Nothing. I'm not naïve. I'm not stupid.

Yes, we got that message through our thick skulls
whether the knowledge was delivered
the time we weren't believed
or that other time we were advised not to make a fuss
or when that bill didn't pass and that MP made a joke of it
or maybe the moment we understood the police weren't there
to protect us that day. Or that day. Or that day
we realised we'd internalised the expectation
that we will continue to set light to candles, but not petrol,
and that our fists will always be too full of flowers to fight.

We know our screams are silenced
by the soft pillow over our faces.
We know our tears serve no purpose
other than for the photographer to get his shot,
so he can leave this crowd of women and go home early.

We know. Suzy. Rachel. Naomi.
We know. Lin. Amelie. Milly.
We know. But we go anyway,
because we also know
that not going
feels a little bit worse.

Wrap up warm, it's cold out there.

this is the time

this is not the time
for prayers and petitions
for pussyhats and placards
this is not the time
for candles and carnations
for comfort and crying
catharsis is needed but
this is not the time

this is not the time
for letters and lawyers
for listening and learning
this is not the time
for fractures and factions
for fantasies of fairness
things may get better but
this is not the time

this is not the time
for solitude and sadness
for symbols and silence
this is not the time
for countering with caring
for killing with kindness
when we're dying but told that
this is not the time

this is the time
to snuff out our candles
and convene in the darkness
this is the time
to snip open our skirt seams
and snap off our high heels
we need to run faster
and this is the time

this is the time
to lay down our flowers
and raise up our freed fists
this is the time
to stop loving but losing
learn Lysistrata, Lorena
power's not given but taken
and this is the time

this is the time
to dust off wits and weapons
to convince kith and kin
this is the time
to get up though we're tired
to rise up and resist
all we feared is here
and this is the time

how did you get so strong?

I got up off the floor, out of the road, and away from the voice that said I can't.

I listened to *Little Earthquakes* by Tori Amos, *Get Better* by Frank Turner, and to my instincts again.

I watched Lisbeth Salander, Buffy Summers, and the ending of *Dogville* on repeat.

I walked through epic thunderstorms, kink markets, and the exposed landscapes of my childhood.

I read feminist politics, and Greek mythology, and people's expressions when they talk.

I took up silversmithing, and weightlifting, and space.

I grew flowers, and children, and the hottest chillies you can imagine.

I constructed IKEA furniture, backstories for inanimate objects, and boundaries I wouldn't cross any more.

I wore little black dresses, pink dungarees, and an expression that said *I will stand my ground here.*

I cried over injustices, over broken hearts, and over the best dessert I ever ate.

I drank eight pints of water, spinach-based juices, and champagne on the worst days.

I committed to spin classes, seven-step skincare, and emotionally-safe sex.

I travelled to Palestine, and Moscow, and back to the places where old ghosts needed laying to rest.

I surrounded myself with friends who would have my back, call me on my bullshit, and eat cat food just to win an argument with me.

I loved women, and men, and myself.

I refused to be too cool to hold hands, or like Taylor Swift, or believe we can make a difference.

And after it all, here I am. Here this is.
And here you are.
And everything you needed to do to make it here too.

I see you.
I've got you.
We're going to be ok.

notes and acknowledgements

Thanks to *Ink Drinkers, iamb, Hearth & Coffin* and Fly on the Wall Press, who published versions of some of these poems.

The quotes in 'four songs' are taken variously from the Bible (Book of Isaiah, Chapter 47 and Book of Jeremiah, Chapter 21) and from David Gray's 1999 album 'White Ladder'.

The title 'at the hospital for ill fairy tales' is taken from the poem 'Findings' by Tasos Leivaditis, trans. N. N. Trakakis.

Thanks to Colin Bancroft for the lovely home with Nine Pens, and to the writers who gave me the best notes: Glyn Maxwell, Rebecca Tamás, Iain Whiteley and (always) Matt Morrison.

For the songs: Grace Petrie, Rachael Sage and Thea Gilmore. For the resilience: Joe Bua-Otema and Yolanda Renjifo.

For their support and encouragement - and the time to write - my thanks to my family: Gretel and Griffin, James and Alice.

Love, respect and gratitude to Nikos Kaplis, who reminded me I like poetry and believed in this project from the start.

For my BFF, Alice MacLachlan, and all the other real-life goddesses I'd hex with over brunch any time: Carolyn Pedwell, Katie Ghose, Katharine Braddick, Steph Lofts, Florence Hunter and Zoë Waxman. We're going to be ok.

Milton Keynes UK
Ingram Content Group UK Ltd.
UKHW040948041123
431884UK00005B/178

9 781739 151775